# *Maharana Kumbha*

# *Maharana Kumbha:*

## Sovereign, Soldier, Scholar.

BY

HAR BILAS SARDA, F.R.S.L.

GYAN

*Published by*

GYAN

Gyan Publishing House
5, Ansari Road
Daryaganj, New Delhi-110002
Phone: 011-47034999, 9811692060
E-mail: books@gyanbooks.com

*Distribution Network*
gyanbooks.com
India, USA, Canada, UK, Australia



ISBN: 978-93-6208-463-7 (HB)
First Published, 1917

2nd Impression 2024

*Printed at:* Gyan Press, Delhi.



**MAHARANA KUMBHA**
Author: HAR BILAS SARDA

# *Maharana Kumbha:*

## *Sovereign, Soldier, Scholar.*

BY

HAR BILAS SARDA, F.R.S.L.,

MEMBER OF THE ROYAL ASIATIC SOCIETY OF GREAT BRITAIN AND IRELAND FELLOW OF THE ROYAL STATISTICAL SOCIETY OF LONDON; FELLOW OF THE STATISTICAL SOCIETY OF BOSTON, UNITED STATES, AMERICA, &C., AND AUTHOR OF AJMER: HISTORICAL AND DESCRIPTIVE.

---

AJMER:

SCOTTISH MISSION INDUSTRIES COMPANY, LIMITED.

1917.

Dedicated

by

Kind Permission

to

The Honourable Sir Elliot Graham Colvin.

K.C.S.I., C.S.I., I.C.S.,

Agent to the Governor-General for Rajputana,

and

Chief Commissioner, Ajmer-Merwara.

# CONTENTS.

## ILLUSTRATIONS

# FOREWORD.

Colonel Tod's Monumental work, the Annals and Antiquities of Rajasthan, published in the thirties of the last century, was written at a time when the history of Rajputana was practically a sealed book to the public. Nearly a century has since passed, yet such are the intrinsic merits of "that wonderful work," that it still remains the chief source to which a student of Rajput history has to turn for enlightenment and knowledge.

Though historical research has made little progress in Rajputana during the last hundred years, yet epigraphic finds, discovery of manuscripts, coming to light of some of the historical records of Rajput States since the publication of the *Annals and Antiquities of Rajasthan,* have thrown fresh light on many obscure points, and though several sources of information in Rajputana have not yet been tapped, nevertheless a student of history with a little diligence can now get a fairly accurate knowledge of the history of this part of the country during the last 500 years.

Materials for such knowledge, however, lie scattered in various journals, books, pamphlets, manuscripts museums and private art and coin collections. To bring together and make proper use of all this material is no easy task but the labour of a lifetime. Probably the time has not yet come for the accomplishment of this most important work. Till then no proper and complete history of India can be written, because the influence of Rajputana on Imperial affairs and the Court at Delhi and Agra during the Moghul and pre-Moghul times was a factor of great importance and often of decisive consequence.

In the meantime, short accounts of important personages, who have played memorable parts in the history of this historic province would not be devoid of interest to the public. The present volume is the first of a series of monographs which I hope, health and time permitting, to write on some of those great men who, by their character and achievements, have made the name *Rajput* a synonym for chivalry and heroism, and the history of this province the brightest page in the history of Mediæval India.

In writing this book, I have made full use of all the inscriptions of the time of Maharana Kumbha and his father, Mokal—many of them unpublished—the Kumbhalgarh, the Chitorgarh (Tower of Victory) the Ranpur, the Eklingji temple and the Mount Abu inscriptions, as well as of the celebrated work Eklinga Mahatamya, the only known manuscript copy of which is in the possession of Rai Bahadur P. Gauri Shankar Ojha—to whom my obligations are due for having allowed me free use of it, as well as of the inscriptions in his possession. I have also made use of a manuscript History of Marwar, Mehta Nainsi's Chronicles (a rare manuscript) Kumbha's Commentaries on *Gita Govinda* and Kaviraja Shyamaldas' *Vir Vinod.*

AJMER, HAR BILAS SARDA.
*1st January 1917.*

# CHAPTER I.

## THE GUHILOT FAMILY OF MEWAR.

MAHARANA KUMBHAKARANA or Kumbhá, as he is popularly called, was one of the greatest of the Maharanas who have ruled in Mewar. The *Surya Vamsha* is the most famous of the ruling families of India, and the most celebrated of its many branches is the Guhilot or Gehlot family, which has ruled Mewar without a break for nearly fourteen centuries. It has produced some of the greatest and most powerful of the kings that have made the name of Rajputana resplendent in the annals of India.

Inspired by the highest patriotism, ever upholding *Dharma*, though surrounded by powerful foes and faced with insuperable difficulties, enduring without flinching untold suffering, and overcoming all by a self-sacrifice and heroism which have wrung the highest praise from their bitterest foes, they have made the pages of history a continuous record of high inspiration and noble purpose. Their immortal deeds, their chivalrous character, their high ideals, their elevated and noble patriotism have placed them at the head of the Hindu nation and earned for them the richly-deserved title of *Hindua Suraj*, "the Sun of the Hindus."

"It has rarely occurred in any country," says the great historian of Rajputana, Col. Tod, "to have possessed successively so many energetic princes as ruled Mewar through several centuries." Jaitra Singh Hamir, Kumbhá, Sángá, Pratáp, Ráj Singh are names that will shine bright throughout the ages, and will be revered so long as chivalry is not despised, patriotism not discarded and valour not condemned.

Maharana Kumbha ascended the throne of Mewar in A.D. 1433, in the renowned fortress of Chitor and ruled till A.D. 1468, a period of nearly 35 years, which is one of the most prosperous and important in the history of Mewar. His character and achievements are thus summed up in a sentence by

Maharana Pratap of Mewar

the illustrious Colonel J. Tod. He says: "All that was wanting to augment her (Mewar's) resources against the storms which were collecting on the brows of Caucasus and the shores of Oxus, and were destined to burst on the head of his grandson, Sángá, was effected by Kumbha, who with Hamir's energy, Lakha's taste for arts, and a genius comprehensive as either and more fortunate, succeeded in all his undertakings, and once more raised the crimson banner of Mewar upon the banks of the Caggar, the scene of Samarsi's defeat." [1]

Kumbhá was the eldest son ofRáná Mokal by his Parmár Queen, Sobhágya Devi,[2] daughter of Rájá Jaitmál Sánkhla, and thus united in himself the fine qualities of these two of the royal races of India, the culture of the one and the chivalry of the other.

[1] Tod's Annals and Antiquities of Rajasthan, Vol. I, p. 287.

[2] Chitorgarh *Kirtistambha* Inscription, verse 179. Also Kumbhalmer inscription of Kumbha. As a girl she was called Mayá Kanwar.

# CHAPTER II.

## RANA KSHETRA SINGH, LÁKHÁ AND MOKAL.

KUMBHA'S great grandfather, Rana Kshetra Singh, who ruled Mewar from A.D. 1364 to A.D. 1382, was the son and successor of the celebrated Ráná Hammir. He greatly enlarged the kingdom. He captured Ajmer and Jaházpur, re-annexed Mándalgarh, Mandsor, and the whole of the Chappan to Mewar. He obtained a victory over the King of Delhi,[1] who was utterly defeated at Bakrole. Kshetra Singh took the King of Gujrat prisoner in a battle. The Kumbhalgarh Inscription says that "he captured Zafar Khan, King of Pátan" (the first independent Sultan of Gujrat),[2] and

[1] Tod's Annals and Antiquities of Rajasthan, Vol. I, p. 274. The Chitorgarh Inscription of Rana Kumbha says (verse 22) that Kshetra Singh "destroyed a Mussalman army near Chitor and the enemy fled to save themselves." He thus put an end to the pride of the Mussalman King. See also the Kumbhalgarh Inscription of Maharana Kumbha.

[2] Lane Poole's Muhammadan Dynasties of India, p. 376.

"the Khán remained in imprisonment with other Rajas; Rana Kshetra Singh defeated and killed Ami Shah (V. 200) and the Mussalman ruler of Malwa trembled in his dreams when he saw the Ráná. He defeated many Rájás and humbled the pride of the ruler of Malwa."

Rana Kshetra Singh was succeeded by his son Rana Laksha Singh or Lákhá, who was one of the most successful of the Maharanas and reigned from A.D. 1382 to A.D. 1397.

He extended his dominions [1] by the subjugation of Merwara and the destruction of its chief stronghold, Beratgarh, on the ruins of which he founded Badnor. It was in his time that the tin and silver mines of Jawar were discovered in the country conquered from the Bhils by his father. With the revenues thus augmented he rebuilt the palaces and temples destroyed by Ala-ud-din, excavated reservoirs and lakes, raised immense ramparts to dam their waters, and constructed a number of forts. He conquered the

[1] Tod's Rajasthan, Vol. I, p. 274.

Sánkhlá Rajputs of Shekháwáti (Nágarchál territory). and, like his father, defeated the royal army of the Delhi Sultan at Badnor.

He conquered *Tristhali* from the Musalmans[1] and the hill fort of Vardhan from the Meds (Mers).[2]

"He carried the war to Gaya, and in driving the barbarian from this sacred place," lost his life.[3] According to the Chitorgarh *Kirtistambha* Inscription he forcibly put an end to the pilgrim tax at Gayá.

Many years before his death, while he was still adorning the throne of Mewar and embellishing the country, an incident occurred which, while illustrating the thoughtless character of the Rajput, gave rise to an event which compromised the right of primogeniture to the throne of Mewar, and in the words of Colonel Tod, "proved more disastrous in its consequences than the arms of either Mughals or Mahrattas."

Lakha was advanced in years, and his sons

[1] The Kumbhalgarh Inscription of Maharana Kumbha.

[2] *Ibid.* Also Chitorgarh *Kirtistambha* Inscription.

[3] Tod's Rajasthan, Vol. 1, p. 275.

established in suitable domains, when the cocoanut came from the Rao of Mandawar (Mandor) to affiance his daughter, Ran Mal's sister, to the heir of Mewar. "When the embassy was announced, Chondá, the heir of Mewar, was absent, and the old chief was seated in his chair of state surrounded by his court. The messenger of hymen was courteously received by Lákhá, who observed that Chondá would soon return, and take the gage; 'for,' added he, drawing his fingers over his moustachios, 'I don't suppose you send such playthings to an old grey-beard like me.' This little sally was applauded and repeated. Chondá offended at delicacy being sacrified to wit, declined to accept the symbol which his father had even in jest supposed might be intended for himself." Thinking that his father still had a secret longing for married life, Chondá, made up his mind that Lákhá should himself accept the symbol. He asked Ran Mal, who happened to be at Chitor at the time, to invite him to a feast, and then insisted on Ran Mal agreeing to give his sister to the Maharana before joining his festive board. Ran Mal would not agree to this, and the night neared the morn with the festive board still deserted.

Not knowing how else to get out of the difficulty, Ran Mal hit on a proposal which he thought would turn the tables on Chondá. He suggested through Cháran Chandan *khadiyá* that Chondá should renounce his right to the throne of Chitor in favour of an issue of the Rana by his sister. Chondá, whose sole desire was to gratify the supposed wish of his father, unhesitatingly agreed to this. The marriage was celebrated and Mokal was the issue of this union.

When Mokal was but five years of age, "Lákhá resolved to signalize his finale by a raid against the enemies of his faith and to expel the barbarian from the holy land of Gaya. When war was made against their religion by the Tatar proselytes of Islam, the Sutlaj and the Caggar were as the banks of the Jordan—Gaya, their Jerusalem, their holy land; and if the destiny filled his cup, the Chief Hindu was secure of his beatitude (Moksha), and borne from the scene of probation in celestial cars by the Apsaras, was introduced at once into the realm of the Sun.

Ere, however, the Rana of Chitor journeyed to this bourne he was desirous to leave his throne unexposed to civil strife. The subject of succession had never been renewed; but discussing with Chonda his warlike pilgrimage to Gaya, from which he might not return, he sounded him by asking what estates should be settled on Mokal. The 'throne of Chitor' was the honest reply; and to set suspicion at rest, he desired that the ceremony of installation should be performed previous to Lakha's departure. Chondá was the first to pay homage and swear obedience and fidelity to his future sovereign." [1]

Lakha had the Holy-land freed from the yoke of the Afghan but lost his life in the enterprise. When news of this event reached Chitor, Mokal's mother prepared to become *sati*. Chonda appeared and dissuaded her from her resolution saying that Mokal was a child, and she, the Queen-mother, must watch over the welfare of the Rana. The Queen did not expect this steadfast fidelity from Chonda. She praised

[1] Tod's Rajasthan, Vol. I, p. 277.

his unexampled conduct and declared that he (Chonda) should ever have the first place in the Council, and no grant by the Rana should take effect till it was confirmed by him. "This is still maintained, and in all grants the lance of the Salumbra still *precedes* the monogram of the Rana."

This assignment of the first place in the Council and a recognition of the premier position amongst the vassalage of Mewar, became the cause of its ruin, when, in the 18th century, the descendants of Chonda strenuously worked to maintain the position thus assigned to Chonda, but forgot the self-sacrifice of that great man, and proved incapable of following in the footsteps of the illustrious founder of their family, when their country had need of those qualities of head and heart, which are so gloriously illustrated in the life of Chonda.

Mokal thus came to the throne in 1397 A.D. and maintained the traditions of the house in defeating in the field of Raipur, Mohammad Tughluq, the king of Delhi. Rana Mokál "overran *Sapadalaksha*

(Ajmer), and took Sámbhar from the Sultan of Delhi. The rulers of Jálor (Jabalipur) trembled before him; and the King of Delhi became anxious about his territory.[1]" Mokal defeated Sultan Firoz Khan of Nagor [2] and Mohamed Gazni Khan, the third Ghori Sultan of Mandu, and killed their elephants. Mokal rebuilt the great temple of Samádhishwar, near the 'Tower of Fame' at Chitor and a beautiful tank at *Papamochana tirtha.* [3]

He overcame the Nishadas and struck terror into the hearts of the Turushkas (Turks or Moslems).

Mokal was assassinated by his two uncles, Cháchá and Mairá, the natural sons of Rana Kshetra Singh by a handsome girl named Karmān, daughter of Medni Mal carpenter—a class still well-known for the physical beauty of their women. Cháchá and Mairá had risen

[1] The Kumbhalgarh Inscription of Rana Kumbha.

[2] *Vide* Samadhishwar Mahadeva Temple Inscription of *Magh sud* 3rd, Thursday, S. 1485 (A.D. 1429).

[3] *Ibid.* He presented a temple of Devi with an image of a lion made of all the metals, and a temple of Vishnu, with a gold image of Garuda.

to be captains in the army of Mokal and thus excited the jealousy of some of the Chiefs of Mewar, who, wishing to humiliate them, had recourse to a trick which cost the Rana his life.

One day in A.D. 1433, while the Rana was encamped at Madáriá and was seated in a grove with his chiefs around him, he enquired the name of a particular tree. Hárá Máldeva, feigning ignorance, whispered to him to ask either of the brothers. Not perceiving the insinuation involved in the question, Mokal artlessly asked, "*Kákáji* (uncle) what tree is this?" The question reminded them of their mother's origin and was taken to be an insult. They vowed vengeance. Ran Mal, who was at Chitor at the time, also came to know that Cháchá and Mairá meditated treachery. News of their unsuccessful attempt to gain over Malesi Dodiá reached Ran Mal and he warned the Maharana that an attempt on his life was imminent. The Maharana, however, took no heed of it. An occasion soon presented itself to the traitors for carrying into execution their nefarious design.

Besides seven sons, Mokal had a daughter named Lálbái, who had been married to Achal Singh, the Kheechi Chief of Gagroon. Achal Singh had at the *Hathléwa'* demanded and received from the Rana the pledge of succour on foreign invasion. Hoshang of Malwa, having attacked Gagroon, Achal Singh sent his son, Dhiraj Singh, to the Rana demanding fulfilment of his pledge. Mokal started from Chitor and Sánwaldas, the Raja of Idar, joined him on the way. Chάchá and Mairá, who had won over Máhpá Panwár and some other minor chiefs to their cause also accompanied the Rana on this expedition. Sánwaldas, owing to his intimacy with Chάchá, came to know of the plot and warned Mokal, but Mokal only laughed at the idea. One night while the Maharana was encamped at Bágor, the two traitors, collecting a small force, surprised the Rana in his tents. The Rana's attendants prepared to defend him. Nine men stood by the Rana, five by his Queen Hádiji and five by Malesi Dodiyá, the gatekeeper of the Palace. The Maharana, Rani Hadiji and Malesi defended themselves bravely but were killed, not, however, till they had slain 19 of the conspirators and wounded Cháchá and Máhpá. Seventy of the Rana's men, including Sánwaldas, were slain. Kanwar Kumbhá escaped with difficulty. Going to the house of a Patel who owned two of the fleetest horses in Mewar, he mounted one and, killing the other at the suggestion of the Patel to baffle pursuit, escaped. The traitors, who were looking out for Kumbhá, were at the Patel's house soon after his departure, but seeing one steed lying dead and the other gone, they returned to their tents. The traitors thence went to Chitor and proclaimed Cháchá as Maharana of Mewar, Mahpá becoming his Diwán.

When the news of this tragedy reached Ráo Ran Mal, the brother of Mokal's mother Háns Bái, this valiant Rathor king, remembering the debt of gratitude he owed to Mokal, with whose help he had recovered the throne of Marwar—his rightful inheritance usurped by his younger brother Sattá in A.D. 1409—threw off the turban he was wearing, put on a *phentá* (a piece of cloth generally worn when in mourning) and swore that he would put the turban on his head only when he had revenged Mokal by slaying his murderers. Leaving Nagor he came to Chitor and defeated the traitors, who with their families fled to the hills of Pái Kotrá, and throwing themselves into the stronghold of Rátákot, fortified it. Ran Mal, after placing Kumbha on the throne of Mewar, started in pursuit of the traitors towards the Pai hills. Arriving there, he made several attempts to reach the fortress, but so steep was the hill and so rugged the path that led up to the fort that Ran Mal failed to achieve his object.

During the reign of Mokal, Ran Mal had, whilst living at Chitor, killed a Bhil zamindar of a village situated at the foot of the Pái hills. The sons of this zamindar with other Bhils, were now actively assisting Cháchá and Maira against Ran Mal. Finding that without the assistance of the Bhils he could not reach the fort, Ran Mal went unattended to the house of the Bhil he had murdered. His widow was at home and the sons had gone out. He addressed her as sister, greeted her, and sat down. The Bhil woman said: "Brother, you did us great wrong, but as you have come to our house, we cannot do anything to you now." Hearing the approach of her sons, the Bhil lady asked Ran Mal to go inside the house, and had his horse tethered at the back of it. Her five sons now arrived and sat down to dinner. She asked them what they would do to Ran Mal if he should come to their house. The young men exclaimed, "Do what! we will kill him." The eldest, however, said "Mother, if he comes to our house, we will say nothing to him." The lady praised her son's noble sentiments and called to Ran Mal to come out. Ran Mal came out. The Bhils received him courteously and asked him why he had come there to be killed. He replied: "My dear nephews I have taken a vow not to eat bread till I have killed Cháchá and Maira; but with you to assist them, I cannot get at them." The Bhils promised to abstain from rendering any further assistance to Cháchá and Mairá, and to assist Ran Mal in achieving his object. Ran Mal returned to his camp and started next day with 1,140 Gehlots and Rathors to take the fort. On arriving at the foot of the hill, the Bhils advised Ran Mal to wait a few days, as the bypath leading to the fort had been blocked by a lioness who had lately given birth to a cub. Ran Mal said he did not mind that, and went on. Placing his men at suitable points he ascended the hill with 60 men. They commenced the ascent where the parapet was yet low: the path was steep and rugged, and in the darkness of the night each grasped his neighbour's skirt for security. As the party reached a ledge of the rock, the glowing eyeballs of the lioness flashed upon them as she came roaring towards them. Ran Mal ordered his son, Aradakamal, to dispose of the beast. He advanced and buried his poniard in her breast. This omen was superb. They soon reached the summit. Some had ascended the parapet, others were scrambling over when the minstrel slipping, fell, and his drum which was to have accompanied his voice in celebrating the conquest, awoke, by its crash, the daughter of Chácha. Her father quieted her fears by saying it was the thunder and rain of *bhádon*, and told her to fear God only and go to sleep, for their enemies were safe at Kailwá. At this moment the avengers of Mokal rushed in. Ran Mal hurled his spear at the door, and people at once said it was Ran Mal's. Cháchá and Mairá had no time to avoid their fate. Cháchá was cleft in two by Chauhán Sujá, while the Rathor prince laid Mairá at his feet. Ran Mal then went to the quarters occupied by Mahpá Panwár and called him to come out and meet his fate, for he had taken a vow not to attack any one who was in the company of women. At the very first call, Máhpá, unable to face his foe, put on female garments and thus disguised, left the house unmolested. In answer to the second call a Dom woman shouted from inside that the Thákur had put on her clothes and left the house and that she was sitting naked inside. On this, Ran Mal returned and joined his companions. Though Cháchá and Mairá met the fate they richly deserved, Cháchá's son, Ekká, escaped and he and Máhpá made straight for the Court of Mandu, where they found shelter. Ran Mal took Cháchá's daughter to wife, making Cháchá's body serve as a *bajot* to sit on at the ceremony.

He married 500 *Sisodia* girls there to spears, intending to give them to his Rathor followers. The Maharana's uncle, Rághavadeva, the brother of Chondá, did not like this proposal, and on arriving at Delwara removed the maids to his own camp. This added fuel to the fire of jealousy already existing between Rághavadeva and Ran Mal.

Ran Mal preferring the fertile plateau of Mewar to the arid deserts of Marwar took up his residence at Chitor, surrounded himself and the Maharana with Rathors, and took the administration in his own hands. Rághavadeva, who had been left by his elder brother Chondá, on his departure from Chitor during the reign of the late Maharana Mokal, to watch over the safety of the Maharana during his minority, had the same duty to perform now that Rana Kumbhá, Mokal's son, was a minor. Rághavadeva did not approve of the proceedings at the Court, which was now dominated by the Rathors, and not willing to do anything which might be unpalatable to the Dowager Maharani, he silently watched the progress of events. But his existence was a menace to the power of Ran Mal and an obstacle to the success of his contemplated designs. Ran Mal, therefore, resolved to remove him. He sent him a dress of honour, which included an *angarkhá*, the sleeves of which were sewn at the ends. As he was putting it on, his arms became entangled in the sleeves, and he was assassinated by two of Ran Mal's men, who stabbed him with their daggers. Rághavadeva had been beloved throughout Mewar for his high character, courage, manly beauty and patriotism. This murder roused great indignation against the Rathors, and obtained for the victim divine honours and a place amongst the *Pitridevas* of Mewar.

# CHAPTER III.

## Rise of the Kingdoms of Gujrat and Malwa.

The invasion of India by Timur, the flight of Mohammad Tughlaq, and the conquest and sack of Delhi by the invader in A.D. 1398 destroyed the power of the Tughlaq Sultans of Delhi. After Timur's departure to Turkistan, Mohammad Tughlaq returned to Delhi, but he had lost all power and prestige and was a Sultan more in name than in reality. In the opening years of the fifteenth century, Malwa, Gujrat and Nagor, the erstwhile viceroyalties of Delhi threw off their allegiance and declared their independence. And it was with all these kingdoms, then in the heyday of their power and prosperity, that Maharana Kumbhá, about the middle of the fifteenth century, came into collision.

Gujrat had been under the rule of the Baghela branch of the Chaulukyas till the year 1297 A.D., when Sultan Ala-ud-din Khilji of Delhi sent Ulugh Khan to conquer it. The Chaulukyas had succeeded the Cháurá Rajputs, who had founded Anhalwara Pātan, the celebrated Capital of Gujrat. The Monarchy of Gujrat reached the height of its magnificence and power under Siddhráj Jaisingh and Kumár Pál (1094-1175 A.D.), when it triumphed over Malwa, conquered Chitor and defeated the Chohāns of Ajmer.

Gujrat remained a tributary province of Delhi from A.D. 1297 to the year 1407 A.D., when the Viceroy, Zafar Khan, proclaimed his independence and mounted the throne of Gujrat[1] at Birpur, under the title of Muzaffar Shah. Zafar Khan was originally a Hindu named Sadharan of the Tánk tribe (Khatri), and after his conversion to Islam became the head of the kitchen to Sultan Firoz Shah Tughlaq, who eventually appointed him Governor of Gujrat. Muzaffar Shah appointed his brother Shams Khan Governor of Nagor, where he and his descendants ruled for several generations, enjoying the unstinted support of the Sultans of Gujrat. Shams

[1] Lane Poole's Muhammadan India, page 376.

Khan was succeeded at Nagor by his son, Firoz Khan, who was a warrior of some renown. He measured swords with Kumbha's father, Maharana Mokal. He invaded Mewar and defeated the Rana at the field of Jotāyān, near Bandanwara, now a part of the district of Ajmer. Flushed with this success, Firoz Khan advanced into Mewar, but sustaining a disastrous defeat[1] at Jáwar, 20 miles south of Udaipur, returned discomfited to Nagor.

The capture of Nagor in A.D. 1455 by Kumbha brought the Sultan of Ahmedabad into the field against him. With the King of Malwa, the Maharana had come into collision in the early part of his reign. These two kingdoms—the most powerful Mussalman principalities in India at the time—when defeated singly by the Maharana, combined and simultaneously invaded Mewar from the west and the south; but Kumbha, supported by the chivalry of Mewar and inspired by the patriotic valour of the Gehlot Rajputs, vanquished them both.

[1] See Samadhishwar Mahadeva Temple Inscription, at Chitor of *Magh Sud* 3rd, S. 1485 (A.D. 1429).

Till 1310 A.D. (710 H.) Malwa was ruled by Hindus. In that year, Sultan Gyasuddin Balban of Delhi sent an army to Malwa and conquered it. It remained a province under the Sultans of Delhi till, in the reign of Sultan Muhammad II, the son of Firoz Tughlaq, it became an independent monarchy. Dilawar Khan Ghori, whose real name was Hassan, was appointed Governor of Malwa in the reign of Fíroz Tughlaq. On 18th December 1398 A.D. Amir Timur captured Delhi and sacked it on the 28th. Sultan Mohamed Tughlaq, the son of Firoz Tughlaq, fled towards Gujrat, and finding his way barred by the Maharana, who inflicted a defeat on him at Raipur, he turned towards Malwa, where he was welcomed and royally entertained by Dilawar Khan. On Timur's departure, Muhamud Tughlaq returned to Delhi, and in 1401 A.D., Dilawar Khan proclaimed his independence and took up his residence at Dhar.

The kingdom of Malwa thus created continued in existence till the year 1571 A.D., when Akbar made it a province of his empire.

**Emperor Akbar.**

Dilawar Khan was murdered by his ambitious and unscrupulous son, Alp Khan, who mounted the throne under the title of Sultan Hoshung Ghori. Sultan Hoshung Ghori's son was murdered by Mahmud Khan, who ascended the throne under the title of Sultan Mahmud Khilji. During his reign the kingdom of Malwa reached the zenith of its power and prosperity, and it was Sultan Mahmud Khilji that the Maharana challenged to stand the onslaught of the Rajputs.

---

# CHAPTER IV.

## Conquest of Malwa and Capture of Sultan Mahmud Khilji.

As one of the assassins of Mokal, Mahpá Panwár, was sheltered by the Sultan of Mandu, a demand for his person was made by the Maharana, but Mahmud Khilji refused to surrender the refugee. The Maharana prepared for hostilities and advanced to attack Mandu. The Sultan advanced with a powerful army to meet Kumbhá.

Chondá, the elder brother of Rana Mokal, who had resigned the throne of Mewar in favour of Mokal in circumstances which have made his name illustrious in the history of India, had taken up his residence in the Court of Mandu, where the Sultan, Dilawar Khan Ghori, had given him the district of Hallar as a *jagir* for his maintenance. The Sultan now asked Chondá to lead the Mandu army against Ran Mal and take revenge for the murder of Rāghavadeva. The patriotic

Chondá replied that he would gladly have led the army against Ran Mal's Rathors, but that it was against his *dharma* to take up arms against the army of the Maharana. Rather than stay at Mandu, he retired to his *jagir*.

The Maharana's army is said to have consisted of a hundred thousand horsemen and 1,400 elephants. The two armies met in A.D. 1440 between Chitor and Mandsaur, and after a severe engagement, the Sultan's army was utterly routed. The Sultan fled and shut himself up in the fort of Mandu. The Rana's army followed up the victory and laid siege to Mandu. When the Sultan was hard pressed, he told Mahpá that he could keep him no longer. Mahpa mounted his horse and going on to the rampart took a leap out of the fort. His horse was killed, but he was saved. He fled to Gujrat. Kumbha stormed and took the fort. Ran Mal captured Sultan Mahmud Khilji, his army fleeing in all directions. The Maharana returned to Chitor bringing the Sultan captive with him.

To commemorate this great victory, the

Maharana built the great ***Jaya Stambha***—Tower of Victory—in the fortress of Chitor, which still adorns that far-famed stronghold—"this ringlet on the brow of Chitor which makes her look down upon Meru with derision." Before, however, this Tower of Victory was completed the Rana had to face and vanquish the combination of the two most powerful kingdoms in India at the time, those of Gujrat and Malwa, which glorious event is inscribed on the celebrated tower.

Mahmud Khilji remained a prisoner in Chitor for a period of six months, after which he was liberated without ransom, by the magnanimity of the Maharana.[1] "So far from showing any generosity thus shown him," says a historian of Mewar, "he (the Sultan) spent the rest of his life in vain attempts at revenging himself on his conqueror, for which purpose he entered

[1] Tod's Annals and Antiquities of Rajasthan, Vol. I, p. 287. Also the Gazetteer of Udaipur, 1908, p. 17. The place of imprisonment still exists. Beyond the palaces of Bhim and Padmini "within a stone enclosure, is the place where the victorious Kumbha confined the King of Malwa."—Arch. S. Reports, XXIII., p. 112.

into an offensive alliance with his former foe, the Sultan of Gujrat."

The time after Mahmud's defeat was very usefully employed by the Maharana in erecting several forts and generally strengthening the defences of his country. Before, however, we proceed to describe them, we must follow the development of the political situation in Mewar itself.

---

## CHAPTER V.

### Occupation of Marwar.

After the crushing defeat and confinement of the King of Malwa in Chitor, Máhpá Panwár and Ekká, son of Cháchá, fled to Gujrat, but finding no shelter there they came and threw themselves at the feet of the Maharana and sued for mercy. The Maharana, with his usual magnanimity, pardoned them and took them into his service.

Kumbhá was still young, and the success which Ráo Ran Mal had achieved in killing the assassins of Mokal, and in crushing the power, and capturing the person of the King of Malwa had raised the influence and power of the Ráo to a pinnacle whence he exercised undisputed sway in Mewar. Rathors were to be seen everywere in the kingdom, and all positions of confidence and trust as well as of political and military importance, were bestowed on them. This naturally excited the apprehensions of the nobles and Sardárs of Mewar. One day Máhpá plainly told the Maharana that the Rathors were aiming at the throne of Mewar; but the Maharana, aware of his enmity towards Ráo Ran Mal, gave no heed to this warning. Ekká, Cháchá's son, a few days later, while shampooing the Maharana, who was asleep, began to weep. His tears falling hot on the feet of the Maharana woke him, and on being asked the cause of his distress, he repeated the tale Máhpá had told.

The Maharana now began to be a little suspicious of Ran Mal. The young Maharana's *dhāya* (nurse) became fearful of the future, and bursting with indignation at the conduct of the Rathors, demanded of the Rana's grandmother, "if her kin was to defraud her own grandchild of his inheritance."

The Dowager Queen spoke to her brother, and his reply only increased her suspicions, which were further strengthened by the assassination of Rághavadeva, the brother of Chondá. An incident which occurred about that time confirmed those suspicions.

A fair maid of the Queen's, named Bhārmali, with whom Rao Ran Mal was in love, was one evening detained a little longer in the palace and went to him later than usual. He asked the cause of the delay, whereupon she said that she was not her own mistress, and that as soon as those whose servant she was, gave her leave she came to him. The answer annoyed the Ráo, who was drunk. He told her she would soon cease to be a servant, and that those who cared to live in Chitor would have to live as her servants. And, yielding to her seductive charms and female art, Ran Mal, intoxicated with liquor as he was, confessed to her his designs. The loyal maid, next day, related the whole incident to the Queen, who communicated the information to the Maharana. All their hopes for the safety of Mewar and its rightful sovereign now rested in Chondá, and to him they at once turned for help. He was apprised of the danger to his country and was asked to come and save it. Chondá, who had been a silent but not inattentive spectator of the dangerous game that was being played in the land of his birth, lost no time in coming to the assistance of the Maharana. He sent 200 of his followers, hunters by profession, to visit their families in Chitor, and while there to ingratiate themselves in the favour of the gatekeepers of the fortress. The young Maharana was asked to descend daily from the fort with a retinue to give feasts to the surrounding villages, and to hold the feast on the Diwáli day at Ghosoonda. The day arrived: the feast was held at Ghosoonda, and night came, but no Chondá arrived. With heavy hearts, the nurse, the Purohit and others started homewards, and had reached the eminence called Chitori when forty horsemen passed them at full gallop, and at their head was the chivalrous Chondá, who, by a secret sign, paid homage to his nephew and sovereign. Chonda and his band reached the Rámpol Gate unnoticed, but here they were challenged. They said they were neighbouring chieftains and had the honour to escort the Maharana home. But the main body, of which this was the advance, presently coming up, the stratagem was discovered. Chonda unsheathed his sword, and at his well-known shout, the hunters were speedily in action. The Bhatti chief in charge of the principal post of Chitor, was killed, though not before he had launched his dagger at Chonda and wounded him.

The old Rao of Mandor now began to scent danger. Fearing surprise, he sent his sons Jodhá (who later founded Jodhpur), Kándhal and others to live in the *taleti*, at the foot of the hill on which the fortress is situated, and told them to be always on their guard and never to come up to the fort even if they should receive a message in his name. Prompted by Chondá, the Maharana asked Ran Mal to call Jodhá and Kándhal to reside in the fortress, but the Rao made some excuse or other. Chondá and the Maharana now decided to rid the fortress of the Rathors.

Bhármali, the Queen's handmaid, one evening in *Asárh*, S. 1500 (1443 A.D.) plied the Rao with liquor. When the old chief was drunk, Bhármali, who had been compelled to his embrace, tied him well to the bed with the big turban he wore. The Rao was only roused to a sense of his danger when Máhpá Panwár, Ekká, son of Cháchá, and others arrived. In his rage, by a sudden desperate movement he got on his legs with the pallet behind him, and roared like a caged lion unable to free himself from the meshes of the turban that tied him to the pallet. Finding all arms removed, he got hold of a brass *lotá*, and with this he killed 3 of his 17 assailants ere he was killed. Máhpá fled as soon as Ran Mal got on his feet. The other Rathors in the fortress, including Randhir, brother of Ran Mal, Sattá Bhati, son of Lunkaran, and Randhir Suráwat, were surprised and slain. Ran Mal was of herculean build. His gigantic stature and the force of his blow were well known in Rajputana. Seeing the state of affairs a *Dom* in the service of Ran Mal, got on to the wall of the fortress and in a loud voice, cried out :—

थांका रणमल्ल मारिया, जोधा भाग सके तो भाग।

"Your Ran Mal has been killed : Jodhá run for your life if you can."

Jodhá and his 700 Rathors saddled their horses, took up their arms and leaving

Bheem, who was too drunk to move, sprang into their saddles and made for Marwar. Chonda, with the memory of the murder of his brother Rághavadeva fresh in his mind started in pursuit with ten thousand Gehlots. A running fight ensued between the Rathors and the Sesodias. There were several encounters.[1] Jodhá had not gone far when Chonda came up and a fight took place at Kapásan. Jodhá, after losing 200 men and killing 400 of the enemy, slipped away. Barjang Bhimawat, Chardá and Chand Rao, sons of Aradakamal (Ran Mal's son), Rana Pitha Rájáwat, Shivaraj, Poorná Bháti, Barisál and others gave up their lives defending Jodhá. Jodha reached Mándal, where Kandhal joined him, and the two brothers continued their flight towards Marwar. They reached the Someshwar Pass in the hills which divide Marwar from Mewar with only a hundred horsemen. Chondá soon came up, and to prevent the Rathors escaping into Marwar made a furious attack on them. The Rathors collected round Jodhá and Kándhal

[1] The Jodhpur *khyat* mentions encounters at Chitori, Satkhamba, Kanawaj, Kapasani and Kélwa.

to save them. Both the Sisodiás and the Rathors dismounted and engaged in a hand-to-hand fight. Out of the 100 horsemen that reached the Pass, Jodhá crossed it with but seven. With this remnant of the 700 horsemen with whom he had left Chitor, Jodhá set foot on the soil of Marwar. He owed his safety to the fleetness of his steed.

Chondá, however, did not give up the pursuit, and arrived at Mandawar (Maṇdor) close on Jodhá's heels. Jodhá unable to make a stand there passed by it. Relying on the aid of the Bhátis of Poogal and Bikampur he took up his abode at the village Kāhuni, ten miles from Bikaner.

The Rana's forces took possession of Marwar and established *thánás* all over the land. Akho Sisodia was appointed Governor of Mandor, Ahádo Hingolo and Mehtá Rayangar were also attached to this fort. Ráwat Rághavadeva, son of Hansmal Chondawat, was given Sojat as *jagir* and was made Thánádar of Chokri. Bháti Banbir, Chohán Jassá of Sachore and the son of Firoz Khan of Nagor were also attached to this

Thánä. Narbad, son of Ran Mal's younger brother Sattá, to whom Rana Mokal had given a Jágir with an annual rental of Rs. 1,00,000—Káyaláná—when Ran Mal was placed on the throne of Mandor in 1409 A.D., remained loyal throughout these transactions, and the Maharana increased his *jagir* by further bestowing on him an estate yielding an income of Rs. 50,000 a year. He took up his abode at Bassi. The year 1443 A.D. thus saw the expulsion of the Rathors from Chitor and the passing of Marwar into the possession of the Maharana.

---

# CHAPTER VI.

## Rao Jodha Recovers Marwar.

After a year's stay at Kahuni, Jodha began to raid Mandor. His raids always cost him men and horses without bringing him any profit. One day, returning from his raid, Jodhá came to a village and put up at the house of one Rákan Jat. The mistress of the house placed before Jodhá a *tháli* (plate) full of hot *ghát* (porridge). Jodhá at once thrust his hand into the centre of the porridge to take a morsel, and as the porridge was burning hot, Jodhá burnt his fingers. Seeing this and not knowing who the stranger was, the Játni said: "Brother, thou art as devoid of sense as Jodhá is." Jodhá was astonished to hear this remark and asked the lady why she thought Jodhá was without sense. The Játni replied that want of sense in Jodhá was clear from the fact that instead of raiding the out-lying country, he always went straight to attack Mandor, which was garrisoned by the Rana; and thus at every encounter he lost horses and men without gaining his object. "And thou, too, my brother," added the lady, "lacketh sense inasmuch as thou putteth thy hand straight into the centre of the porridge and burneth thy fingers. If thou wouldst but begin with the porridge near the edge which is not so hot, thou shouldst have by and by the porridge in the centre of the plate too, as it is not going to run away."

Jodhá took this advice to heart and gave up going towards Mandor and began to raid the country around. This brought him plunder, and he got around him a body of horsemen. His brothers also grew up and began to assist him. With the help of the Bhátis of Kelhan, where he had married, he began to raise disturbances in the country. He was, however, seriously handicapped by want of horses and lack of money. There was famine, too, in the land and grain was scarce.

While Jodhá was thus roaming homeless in Marwar, his country being in the Maharana's possession, an incident occurred which roused him and put fresh energy into his activities. The Dowager Queen of Mewar, Rao Ran Mal's sister, sympathising with Jodhá in his forlorn state, one day begged the Maharana to restore Mandor to the young Rao, telling him how Ran Mal had come to Chitor to help the Maharana at a critical time, slain Cháchá and Mairá, defeated the Mussalmans, raised the credit of Mewar, and was killed there, and that his son Jodhá was now wandering in the jungles, homeless and hopeless. Such, said the lady, was the reward for services rendered to Mewar. The Maharana replied that Ran Mal had murdered Rághavadeva, Chondá's brother, which Chonda could never forget, and that he, for fear of wounding Chondá's feelings, could not do anything to help Jodha, but promised that if Jodhá should take Mandor he would not molest him. Thus assured, the old lady sent a confidential messenger, a *Cháran* named Dulá, to Jodhá to communicate to him the views of the Maharana and to encourage him to make an effort and take Mandor.

Cháran Asiá Dulá went in search of Jodhá, and eventually reaching the village

Bhadang, in the jungles of Padává, in the sandy desert of Marwar, he found him with his fifty horsemen and some foot followers in the act of satisfying their hunger with the *bájri* growing in the fields. The message from the Dowager Queen of Mewar acted like a powerful tonic on him, and he set about collecting means to effect his purpose. He went straight to Ráwat Lunkaran of Satráwa, who had 500 horses in his stables, and appealed to his patriotism, and reminded him of his duty to his kindred and asked for 200 horses. Lunkaran declined to give the horses, saying that he held his fief from tha Maharana, who would deprive him of the land if he should give him assistance. Disappointed by the Ráwat, Jodhá went to the Thakuráni, who was a sister of Jodhá's mother. She was a Bhatyáni lady, a class well known amongst the Rajputs for wisdom and foresight. Seeing Jodhá dejected, she enquired the cause. He told her that the Ráwat had refused him horses of which he was in sore need. The Bhatyáni asked him to cheer up, saying the horses were all his. She sent for the

Ráwat and asked him to put certain valuables in the *Toshákháná;* and when he unlocked the room and went in to deposit the things, the Thakuráni promptly shut the door and locked him in. She then sent one of her maids with Jodhá to the stables with the message that the Ráwat had ordered that the stables were at Jodhá's disposal, and that the keepers were to fully equip any horses that he wished to take away. Jodhá picked out 140 of the best steeds of Satráwá, mounted his Rajputs and marched away. When he was gone the Thakuráni unlocked the door of the Toshá-khána. Ráwat Lunkaran came out boiling with rage, quarrelled with the Thakuráni, scolded his Kámdárs and had the keepers of the stables beaten, but could not get back the horses.[1]

Jodhá thus equipped went to enlist the support of Harbá Sánkhlá, the celebrated cavalier of Rajputana, whose deeds of chivalry

[1] The following couplet refers to the incident :—

ज्यूं ज्यूं कहियो रावत लूणो ।
त्यूं त्यूं लड़े घणेरो लूणो ॥

are sung everywhere in the country. This great man, a *Bála Brahmachári* (he who leads a life of celibacy from childhood), lived a life of simplicity and asceticism, and was ever ready to succour the distressed, help the weak and champion the cause of the oppressed. His generosity was proverbial, his door was open to all who sought his aid, his lance ever ready to go to the assistance of a suppliant with a just grievance. His house, a place of shelter to all who went there, provided unbounded hospitality to the stranger. He had been performing the rite of *Sadāvrat*, at which everyone is shown hospitality and granted his request. Jodhá, with a hundred and twenty followers, arrived when the "strangers' fare" had been distributed. Harbá had a hurried meal of *mujd* boiled with flour, sugar and spices prepared and set before the Ráo and his followers, who enjoyed the pottage and went to sleep.

On waking, they stared at one another, for their moustachios were dyed with the evening's meal. Harbá, however, remarked "that the grey of age was thus metamorphosed into the tint of morn and hope, so would their fortunes become young and Mandor again be theirs."

Thus aided, Jodhá started to recover his patrimony. He first attacked the Maharana's *thánú* of Chaukri. Rághavadeva Rathor with his small following fled, leaving everything behind, and Bháti Ranbir, Rana Visaldeva, Ráwal Indo of the Rana's officers were killed. Jodhá next attacked and took Kosáná, and by rapid marches arrived at Mandor. Two sons of Chándá, Kándhal and Manjá, were in charge of the place. Despising the numbers of the enemy, and ignorant of the fact that the assailants included Harbá Sánkhlá, they descended sword in hand to meet them. But they were overpowered; Kándhal was slain and Manjá took to his horse and fled but was pursued, overtaken and slain on the way. Ahádo Hingolo, Sisodiá Eko and others were also slain. A *chhatri* still marks the place on the Balsamad Lake, near Jodhpur, where Hingolo fell after performing deeds of valour. Chohán Jassá, Harbhám Sindhal, Visaldeva Parmar and the son of Firoz Khan of Nagor fled. Jodhá recovered Mandol. In a few days Jheá also seized Sojat and took up his abode there. Chondá would have invaded Marwar to take *vair* (revenge)—as two sons of his had fallen while Mandor had lost only one chief, Ran Mal—but abstained on learning that the Maharana forbade it. Conscious, however, of the superior power of Mewar, Jodhá sued for peace, and restored the rich province of Godwár [1] to quench the feud. Thus, after 7 years of occupation, Maharana Kumbhá lost Mandor, and Jodhá won it back by the sword.

---

[1] This province remained in the possession of the Maharana for three centuries, only reverting to Marwar in the latter half of the 18th century when, owing to Mahratta aggression, the resources of Mewar reached a low ebb.

# CHAPTER VII.

## WARS WITH THE SULTANS OF MALWA AND GUJRAT.

WE now turn to the foreign relations of Mewar and see how the valiant Maharana not only successfully defended his country against the attacks, first made singly and when thus defeated, made in combination by the Kings of Malwa and Gujrat, then at the zenith of their power and prestige, but carried the war into the countries of his foes, humbled their pride, took from them several forts and cities, extended his dominions on all sides and became the most powerful sovereign of his time in India.

In S. 1499 (A.D. 1442) the Maharana left Chitor to invade Háráváti. Finding Mewar unprotected, the King of Mandu, Sultan Mahmud Khilji, burning with a desire to take revenge and to wipe off his disgrace of A. D. 1440, invaded Mewar, and arriving near Kumbalmer prepared to destroy the temple of Bána Mátá in Kelwárá. A Rajput chieftain named Dip Singh collected his warriors and opposed the Sultan. For seven days Dip Singh successfully repulsed all attempts of the Sultan's army to take possession of the temple. On the seventh day, Dip Singh was killed and the temple fell into the hands of the Sultan. He razed it to the ground, burnt the stone image of the Mátá and used the lime with betel leaves. Flushed with this small success, he started for Chitor, and leaving a part of his army to take the fortress, advanced to attack the Maharana, sending his father, Azam Humayun, towards Mandsaur to lay waste the Maharana's country.

When the Maharana heard of these events, he left Háráváti to return to his dominions and came upon the Sultan's army near Mandalgarh. A battle was fought here without any decisive result.[1] A few days later the Maharana made a night attack on

[1] Ferishta (Vol. IV, p. 210), says the Sultan obtained a victory and the Maharana retired to Chitor, while the historians of Rajputana say that the Sultan was defeated.

the Sultan who was utterly defeated and fled towards Mandu.[1]

To retrieve this disaster, Mahmud set about preparing another army, and four years later, on 20th Rajab H. 850 (Kartik Badi 5th, S. 1503) 11-12 October 1446 A.D., he went towards Mandalgarh with a large army. The Maharana's army attacked him while he was crossing the river Banás, and having defeated him drove him back to Mandu.[2] For about 10 years after this defeat, Mahomed Khilji did not venture to take the offensive against the Maharana.

[1] *Vir Vinod* of Maháinahopádhyárya *Kaviraj* Shamaldas, part I., p. 325. Ferishta says "the Sultan returned without molestation to Mandu."—Vol. IV, p. 210.

[2] *Vir Vinod*, p. 325.—Ferishta, in conformity with the practice of Persian historians, who ignore or try to whitewash defeats and unfavourable issues, says (Vol. IV., p. 210) that the Sultan returned after taking Nazrana. This is obviously far from true. For, had the Sultan obtained a victory and concluded peace after receiving Nazrana, why should he have, as stated by Ferishta (Vol. IV, p. 215), sent Taj Khan with eight thousand cavalry aud 20 elephants to attack Chitor without cause from Bayana, where he had gone immediately after his return to Mandu. Had the Sultan achieved a victory, we should not have found him (as will be seen later) asking the King of Gujrat for help, and proposing to him after his defeat an offensive alliance against the Maharana. Ferishta further says (Vol. IV., p. 222) that

In 1455 A.D. the state of affairs at Ajmer drew his attention to it. This important city—"the heart of Rajputana"—is a place of the greatest strategical importance in Upper India. It stands at the summit of the plateau which marks the highest elevation on the plains of Hindustan. Its political importance is proved by the fact that every power aspiring to dominate the country has first taken possession of it and used it as a ladder to mount to political supremacy in India. Its religious importance is due to the existence of Pushkar in its environs, and the Mausoleum of Khwaja Muinuddin Chishti in the town. The death of Swami Dayanand Saraswati at Ajmer invests the place with peculiar importance in the eyes of reformed Hinduism.

During the reign of Maharana Mokal, Ráo Ran Mal of Mandor wrested this stronghold from the Sultans of Delhi and restored it to Mewar. Acting on the advice of

Mahmud wished to found a town in Mewar and name it Khiljipur, but that as the Maharana tendered a Nazrana he returned to Mandu without doing so. Does this return not plainly show that Mahmud returned foiled in his attempt?

Pancholi Khemsi, Ran Mal sent him out with a picked force of Rathors; and under the pretence of conveying a daughter to the Viceroy of Ajmer, he introduced his men into that renowned fortress, the ancient stronghold of the Chohâns, putting the garrison to the sword and slaying Salim Shah, King of Multan, who had gone on pilgrimage to Ajmer after killing Choondá, father of Ran Mal at Nagor. Khemsi was rewarded with the grant of the township of Khatoo, then lately captured from the Káimkhanees.[1]

In A. D. 1455 Mahmud Khilji having received representations that all Muhammadan religious practices had been forbidden in Ajmer[2] by the Hindu Governor of the place, and receiving promises of help from its Mussalman residents, undertook an expedition against that city. Sending the bulk of his army against Mandsaur to engage the Maharana's forces, he advanced and attacked Ajmer. Gajádhar Singh, the Governor of the fort of Ajmer, defended the fort for four days,

[1] The Jodhpur *Khyat*.

[2] Ferishta, Vol. IV., page 222.

and then, despising the foe's forces, he came out and attacked the Sultan's army. He was killed after performing deeds of valour and slaying numbers of the enemy. As his men were retiring into the fort, the Sultan's men mixed themselves among the Rajputs and entered it also. The Sultan thus obtained possession of the fort but "not without sustaining severe loss."[1] He appointed Khwaja Naimat-ullah as Governor of the fort, with the title of Saif Khan, and himself went towards Mandalgarh.

As he approached the river Banas, the Maharana's army came out of the fort and fell upon the Sultan, who sustained a severe defeat and fled to Mandu.[2]

[1] Ferishta, Vol. IV., page 222.

[2] Ferishta says: "Rana Kumbha, at the head of a body of Rajputs, attacked one flank of the king's army under Taj Khan and sent another body to attack that under Ali Khan. A severe engagement ensued in consequence, when the retreat was mutually sounded. On the following morning the Malwa officers persuaded the king of the necessity of his army retiring into quarters, both on account of the reduced numbers and the wretched state of the camp equipment, now rendered almost useless, which circumstances, together with the approach of the rainy season, induced Sultan Mahmud to return to Mandu."—Briggs Ferishta, Vol. IV, p. 223. Mr. Briggs in a footnote says: "The drawn battle mentioned by the Malwa historians must be deemed a defeat."

The same year (A. D. 1455) Feroz Khan, Sultan of Nagor, died.[1] He belonged to the family of the kings of Gujrat, and was originally Governor of the province of Nagor, under the Sultans of Delhi. He had, however, thrown off his allegiance to Delhi and become independent. On his death, his elder son, Shams Khan, succeeded him, but his younger son, Mujahid Khan, deposed him and prepared to take his life. Shams Khan fled to Rana Kumbhá for shelter [2]and help. Kumbhá, who had long had designs on Nagor, gladly embraced this opportunity of carrying them out, and agreed to place Shams Khan on the throne of Nagor on the condition that he acknowledged Kumbha's supremacy by demolishing part of the battlements of the fort of that place.[3] Shams Khan accepted the terms.[4] The Maharana marched with a large army to Nagor, defeated Mujahid, who fled towards Gujrat, and placed Shams Khan on the *gádi* of

[1] Ferishta, Vol. IV., page 40 (Cal. Edition of 1910).

[2] Bayley's Gujrat, page 148.

[3] Ferishta, Vol. IV., page 40. Also Bayley's History of Gujrat, page 148, footnote.

[4] Ferishta, Vol. IV., page 41.

Nagor, and demanded of him the fulfilment of the condition. As preparations were being made for the demolition of the battlements one of the old Pathan Sardars of Shams Khan cried out: "Would that Firoz had a daughter instead of a son, for even she would not have allowed her father to be disgraced by permitting the dismantling of the fortifications of the fort."[1] On this, Shams Khan humbly prayed to the Maharana to spare the fort just then, for otherwise his nobles would kill him after the Maharana was gone. He promised to demolish the battlements himself later on. The Maharana granted this prayer and returned to Mewar.

No sooner, however, had Kumbhá reached Kumbhalgarh than Shams Khan, instead of demolishing, began to strengthen the fortifications of Nagor. This brought Kumbhá on the scene again with a large army. Shams Khan was driven out of Nagor, which passed into Kumbhá's possession. The Maharana now demolished the fortifications of Nagor and thus carried out his long-cherished design.

[1] Bayley's History of Gujrat, page 148, footnote.

He took away from the treasury of Shams Khan a large store of precious stones, jewels and other valuable things. The *Eklinga Mahatmya* composed during Kumbhá's lifetime, says that he "defeated the King of the Shakas (Mussalmans). put to flight Mashiti (Mujahid ?), slew the heroes of Nágpur (Nagor), destroyed[1] the fort, filled up the moat round the fort, captured elephants, imprisoned Shaka women and punished countless Mussalmans. He gained a victory over the King of Gujrat, burnt the city[2] (Nagor) with all the mosques therein, liberated twelve lakhs of cows from the Moslems, made the land a pasture for cows and gave Nagor for a time to Bráhmans."[3] He carried away the gates of the fort and an image of Hanumán from Nagor, which he placed at the principal gate of the fortress of Kumbhalgarh, calling it the Hanumán Pol.

[1] The Chitorgarh *Kirtistambha* Inscription repeats these facts, and adds that he destroyed "the great mosque built by Sultan Firoz, which showed Moslems the way to Nagor" (verse 19). Verse 22 says "he uprooted the Mussalman tree of Nagor and destroyed it with all its mosques."

[2] Commentary on the *Gita Govinda*, *verses* 60-62, also reiterate these things.

[3] See also Chitorgarh *Kirtistambha* Inscription.

Shams Khan fled to Ahmedabad, taking with him his daughter, whom he gave to Sultan Qutb-ud-din to wife.[1] The Sultan thereupon espoused his cause and sent a large army under Rái Rám Chandar and Malik Gadday to take back Nagor.[2] The Maharana allowed the army to approach Nagor, when he came out, and after a severe engagement, inflicted a crushing defeat on the Gujrat army, annihilating it. Only remnants of it reached Ahmedabad, to carry the news of the disaster to the Sultan.[3]

The Sultan now took the field in person, determined to wrest Nagor back from the Maharana. The Maharana advanced to meet him and came to Mount Ábu.

In S. 1513 (A.D. 1456) the Sultan of Gujrat "despairing of reducing Chitor"[4] arrived near Abu and sent his Commander-in-

[1] Bayley's Gujrat, page 149. Ferishta, Vol. IV., page 41.

[2] Ibid, Bombay Gazetteer, Vol. I., page 242, has Anup Chand Manik and Malik Gadai.

[3] Bombay Gazetteer, page 242, Ferishta Vol. IV., page 41.

[4] Brigg's Ferishta, Vol. IV, page 41.

Chief, Malik Shaaban Imad-ul-Mulk, with a large army, to take the fort of Ábu, and himself marched upon the fortress of Kumbhalgarh. Kumbhá, aware of this plan, came out, attacked and "defeated Imad-ul-Mulk with great slaughter,"[1] and by forced marches reached Kumbhalgarh before the Sultan arrived there.

The Deorás of Sirohi, who had been dispossessed of Ábu by Kumbhá, seized this opportunity when Kumbhá was embroiled with the Sultan of Gujrat, and took possession of Ábu.[2]

Imad-ul-Mulk returned discomfited to the Sultan, and both arrived at the foot of the hill on which is perched the fortress of Kumbhalgarh. The Maharana sallied out of the fortress and attacked and defeated the Sultan,

[1] Bombay Gazetteer, Vol. I, page 242. Also Bayley's History of Gujrat, page 149.

[2] The *Mirati Sikandari* states that the Sultan had the fort evacuated by Kumbha and gave it to the Deoras of Sirohi. *Ferishta*, however, states (Vol. IV, page 41) that the Raja of Sirohi, who was a relation of the Maharana met the Sultan in battle but was defeated, and that the Sultan then went away towards Kumbhalgarh.

who sustained a heavy loss, and hopeless of taking this stronghold, retired[1] to Gujrat.

The Sultans of Malwa and Gujrat, thus defeated by the Maharana, now resolved to combine and invade Mewar. Sultan Qutb-ud-din was met, on his way back to Ahmedabad, by Taj Khan, ambassador from Mahmud Khilji, Sultan of Malwa, who proposed a formal offensive alliance against the Maharana who had destroyed the Mussalman Chiefship of Nagor and had injured them both. The King of Gujrat eagerly listened to the proposal and accepted the terms of the alliance, which was ratified at Chānpāner by Sheikh Nizam-ud-din and Malik-ul-Ulema on behalf of Sultan Mahmud, and by Qazi Hisam-ud-din on behalf of Qutb-ud-din, towards the close of the year A. D. 1456.[2] It was agreed between the two kings that the southern part of Mewar contiguous to Gujrat was to be attached to

[1] Bombay Gazetteer, page 242.

[2] Brigg's Ferishta, Vol. IV, page 42. Bayley's Gujrat, page 150, footnote.

Gujrat; and Mewar proper, Ajmer and Ahirwara, to Malwa.

In pursuance of this treaty, a simultaneous attack was made by the allied kings of Malwa and Gujrat the following year (A.D. 1457). Qutb Shah advanced towards Kumbhalgarh, while Mahmud Khilji advanced towards Chitor and reached Mandsaur. The Maharana wanted to dispose of Mahmud first, but finding that Qutb-ud-din had come near Kumbhalgarh, advanced to meet him first. Qutb-ud-din had chosen a strong position and the Maharana, after an indecisive action, fell back on a better position flanked by his native hills. Qutb-ud-din encouraged, advanced and an engagement took place which lasted for two days. After the first day's engagement, both armies retired to their camps for the night: the dead bodies were cremated or buried, and the wounded were tended. With the break of day the battle was renewed, and as the Maharana's army had the support of the hills behind them, while the Sultan's army was in the open, the latter suffered severely and left the field completely vanquished. The Sultan had to fight hard for his life but eventually retired in safety. Thus, though the Maharana suffered a heavy loss, the Sultan was defeated and returned to Gujrat.[1]

[1] Ferishta (Vol. IV, page 42) says that the Sultan on receiving 14 mds. of gold loaded on two elephants and some other things as presents made peace with the Maharana and returned home! This is Ferishta's way of glossing over a defeat. For Ferishta does not state what "seasonable donation" the Sultan of Malwa, the ally of the Gujrat King, received as his share of the spoils of war or offering of peace. It is hardly possible to believe that this powerful combination of two monarchs, each burning with a desire to completely crush the common foe, should invade the enemy's country from both sides and open the campaign with such confidence and pride, achieve a triumphant victory and yet the net result of it should be the gain to only one of the allies of 14 mds. of gold, two elephants and some nondescript things!!! It is conceivable that the Sultan took with him the spoils of some of the temples destroyed by him and the plunder of Sirohi, and some annalist has described the gold and the nondescript things as nazrana or tribute. The *Mirati Sikandari* says that three months after this, the Maharana invaded Nagor, when Qutb-ud-din again came to Mewar, and after plundering some villages returned to Ahmedabad. It is difficult to believe that if the Maharana had been defeated in this war he would have dared attack Nagor within three months of his defeat, or, that Qutb-ud-din who had been victorious would have retired satisfied after indulging in a little plundering freak without exacting substantial penalty or otherwise taking severe revenge for this presumption on the part of the Maharana. The *Mirati Sikandari*, indeed, says that the Sultan of Mandu returned home, having received from the Rana the district of Mandsaur and several other pargannas adjacent to the territories of Malwa. That the victor should get only a little gold and the spectator whole districts of the country of the vanquished! Another historian, however, comes nearer

The King of Malwa also retired to his territory foiled in his attempt, and was able neither to recover the territory previously conquered and joined to Mewar by Kumbha, nor to conquer any part of the Maharana's country.[1] He had been so often defeated that after this unsuccessful attempt to retrieve his fallen fortunes, he gave up all hope of success against the Maharana, and though he lived for 10 years after this defeat, he never again ventured to invade Mewar.[2]

the truth. "*Tarikhi Alfi* seems rather to intimate that Qutb-ud-din made his own terms and left Mahmud to shift for himself"—Bayley's Gujrat, page 151, footnote. The Commentary on Gita Govind distinctly states that the two kings were defeated and driven out of Mewar by the valiant Maharana.

[1] Ferishta says (Vol. IV, page 224) that Mahmud left for Mandalgarh on 26 Muharram H. 861 (A. D. 1856), and took it on 25 Zilhijj H. 862 (1458 A. D.)! It is further stated that Mahmud advanced towards Chitor on 5 Muharrum H. 863 (1458 A. D.) and sent his son, Prince Ghayas-ud-din, towards Bhilwara, and that the Prince after a severe action took the fort of Kasundi and then returned to Mandu to join his father. Is return home without concluding a triumphant peace a sign of victory?

[2] In S. 1518 (A. D. 1461) Mahmud Khilji did indeed go towards Kumbhalgarh but dared not attack it. He passed on to Dungarpur, received two lakhs from the Raja as *Faujkharch* and returned to Mandu.—Ferishta, Vol. IV, page 225.

Sultan Qutb-ud-din did not long survive[1] this defeat. He died on 25th May A.D. 1459 and was succeeded by Daud Shah in the following year.

About this time, the Hárás of Bundi, Bhándá and Sándá, by a stratagem took possession of Amargarh and gave some trouble to the Rajputs of Mandalgarh. The Maharana, therefore, attacked and took Amargarh, where a large number of the Hárás, including Toghji, the Governor of the Fort, were killed. The Maharana then laid siege to Bundi. Bhándá and Sándá thereupon came to the Maharana, sued for pardon and begged him to spare Bundi. The magnanimous Maharana granted their prayers, and after receiving *Faujkharch* and a fine, returned to Chitor.[2]

The Deorás of Sirohi had thrown off the yoke of the Maharana and taken possession of Ábu in A.D. 1458. The Maharana

[1] Brigg's Ferishta, Vol. IV, page 43.

[2] The Kumbhalgarh Inscription, verse 265, states that the Maharana vanquished the Hárás and received a tribute from them. The Maharana lived for 8 years after the date of the Inscription.

therefore sent an expedition against them, under Narsingh Dodiyá, son of Ráo Shalji, who subjugated them, and, under the orders of the Maharana, constructed a palace and a lake at Ábu.[1]

In S. 1524 (A.D. 1467) reports reached the Maharana that the Mussalmans had begun to kill cows in Nagor. He therefore started with fifty thousand horsemen to attack Nagor. After putting thousands of the enemy to the sword, he captured the fort and carried away a number of elephants, horses and other valuables as spoils of war. The Governor of Nagor fled to the Court of the Sultan of Ahmedabad, who advanced in the direction of Sirohi with a large army, and, after plundering that part of the country, turned towards Kumbhalgarh. The Maharana also advanced with his Rajputs and defeated the Sultan, who turned towards Malwa, and, through that country, returned to his capital.[2]

[1] डोडे राव सिरोही डुजड़ा दलसजड़ा पर बंध दिया।
आबु गिरवर शिखर ऊपरा कुंभे सरवर महल किया ॥

[2] Ferishta places this expedition in A.D. 1458.

# CHAPTER VIII.

## Death of Kumbha.

It is said that an astrologer had told Kumbhá that he would die by the hand of a *Cháran*,[1] whereupon the Maharana expelled the whole community from Mewar and confiscated their lands. Prince Rái Mal[2] befriended them and was involved in their disgrace. He too was banished. A few days before his death, however, the Maharana granted the Chárans permision to return to Mewar.

In A.D. 1468, while Kumbha was one day seated on the edge of a masonry tank, called Mamadeva, near the temple of Kumbhaswami at Kumbhalgarh, which he had built ten years before, his eldest son, Udai Karan, stole up to him and treacherously stabbed him to death.

The motive for this wicked deed might

[1] A community whose members write poetry, remain in attendance on Rajputs, and sing their glorious deeds.

[2] He was the eldest son of Kumbhá by his queen Kumbhaldevi. See Chitorgarh Inscription, v. 180.

be the fear that Rai Mal might be restored to favour and possibly block the miscreant's way to the throne; or, Kumbhá's enemies, unable to overcome him by force, put up his son to do the wicked deed, promising him assistance to get the throne, as was done in the case of Maharaja Ajit Singh of Marwar in the 18th century, when his son, Abhai Singh, was persuaded to get his father murdered. Udai Karan is known in history as "Udo the *Hatiáro*."

Thus, after a reign of 35 years—a reign full of glory and splendour—Kumbhá departed from this world, leaving behind him a name which is honoured in history, and remembered to this day as that of one of the greatest sovereigns who ever ruled in India. The Kumbhalgarh Inscription says that "he was the root of the tree of righteousness, home of virtue and purity, support of wealth, birthplace of truth, abode of prowess, limit of constancy and fortitude, and a representative of *Kalpadruma* (the tree in Heaven which grants all desires). His charities were greater than those of the famous Rájá Bhoj and Karaṇ."

His military achievements, of which any sovereign might be proud, have not often been surpassed in India. His high moral culture prevented him from emulating the deeds of a Timur or an Alla-ud-din Khilji and carrying fire and sword from one end of the country to the other. His genius was equal to achieving far greater feats of military glory than what he accomplished, but his heart, susceptible to the finer feelings of humanity, abhorred all unnecessary bloodshed, ruin and destruction, and he undertook only such military operations as were absolutely necessary for the protection of his country, or as duty enjoined. Fortune constantly smiled on him : he was ever victorous in war. Inscriptions found in Chitor, Kumbhalgarh, Ránpur and Ábu show that he defeated all his enemies, reduced some to be his vassals and incorporated portions of the territories of others with his own. He captured Bundi,[1] Bamodá[2] and conquered Harávati.[3] He

[1] Ranpur Inscription : Achæological Survey of India, Annual Report for 1907-08, pp. 214-17.

[2] Kumbhalgarh Inscription (unpublished) in the Udaipur Museum.

[3] Kaviraj Shyamaldas' *Vir Vinod*. Also Kumbhalgarh Inscription.

captured and incorporated with Mewar, Mandalgarh,[1] Sinhapur,[1] Khatoo, Jaua and Chátsoo,[2] the whole of the district of Toda, and Ajmer.[2] He made the Sapádalaksha[3] countrv, including Sambhar, his tributary, and imposed a tax on the salt[3] produced there. He imposed a tax on the "salt mines" at Didwáná and conquered the city of Naráina.[3] He conquered Naradiyanagar[1] (Narwar), Yagnapur (Jahazpur),[1] Malpura, Yoginipur[1] (Jáwar) and Dungarpur,[1] driving out Ráo Gopal. He burnt down Vrandávatipur and took the hill fort of Gargarát,[1] now called Gangadhār (in Jhallawar), *vide* the Inscription of S. 480 (A.D. 423), Corpus Inscriptionum Indicarum, Vol. III, p. 75. He "burnt Malláranyapur, Sinhapuri, and Ratnpur and destroyed several kings."[1] He killed the enemy and took Mandowar[1] (Mandor). He conquered Ámradádri (Amber) and won the battle of Kotrá[1]

[1] Kumbhalgarh Inscription (unpublished) in the Udaipur Museum.

[2] Ranpur Inscription: Achæological Survey of India Annual Report for 1907-8, pp. 214-15.

[3] Chitorgarh Inscription, a part of which is given in Cunningham's A. S. Reports, Vol. XXIII.

and took Mandalkar (Mandalgarh). He took Giripur. He conquered Sárangpur, taking "numberless Turk women prisoners and humbled the pride of Muhammad, its ruler, who had slain his master and become king of the place."[1] He conquered Hamirpur and married the daughter of its king, Ranbir;[1] captured the hilly country of Vardhamán[1] (Badnor?) from the Mers; took Amrdáchal (?) and conquered the Jankáchal[1] hill from the King of Malwa and built a fort on it; he conquered and occupied the territory of the Sultan of Delhi.[2] He conquered Gokarana Mountain and subjugated the kingdom of Ábu[3] (v. 11) and built Achalgarh[4] on the top of it (v. 12), and made the Deorá chief his vassal;[3] he conquered Gágron[2] (in Kotah), Visalpur[1] and razed to the ground Dhányanagar[1] and destroyed Khandel.[3] He conquered the famous fortress of Ranthambhor.[1] He took away the whole of the wealth and kingdom of Muzaffar[3]

[1] Kumbhalgarh Inscription (unpublished) in the Udaipur Museum.

[2] Ranpur Inscription: Archæological Survey of India, Annual Report for 1907-8, pp. 214-15.

[3] Chitorgarh Inscription, a part of which is given in Cunningham's A.S. Reports, Vol. XXIII.

[4] Ekluiga Mahatmaya.

and humbled his pride (v. 7); conquered Nagor (Marwar)[1] and plundered Jāngaludesha[1] (country west of Ajmer) and incorporated Godwar[2] with his dominions. He repeatedly defeated the kings of Malwa and Gujrat singly and once combined[3] and was called the *Hindu Suratrán*[2] (Sultan), and was presented with the Umbrella of royalty[4] by the kings of Delhi and Gujrat,[4] whose territories he had conquered. He was known to the world as *Rājaguru*,[1] *Dānaguru*, *Chāpaguru* (Master of Archery), and *Sailaguru* (Master of Mountains) and *Parama Guru* (Great Master).[5]

[1] Kumbhalgarh Inscription (unpublished) in the Udaipur Museum. Also Chitorgarh Inscription.

[2] Kaviraj Shyamaldas' *Vir Vinod*.

[3] Chitorgarh Inscription, a part of which is given in Cunningham's A.S. Reports, Vol. XXIII. The Chitorgarh Inscription (verse 17 says that he burnt Gujrat, conquered the ruler of Malwa (Muhammad) and destroyed his pride. Further on (verse 171) Kumbhá is styled Agastyamuni (swallower) of the armies of the Sultans of Gujrat and Malwa.

[4] Ranpur Inscription: Archæological Survey of India, Annual Report for 1907-8, pp. 214-15.

[5] Chitorgarh Inscription, v. 146, where he is called the chief ornament of the kings of the North, East and West.

# CHAPTER IX.

## KUMBHA'S MONUMENTS.

KUMBHA was a great commander and a great king. He not only greatly extended the boundaries of Mewar but immensely strengthened its defences and adorned it with works of art. Colonel Tod says: "He triumphed over the enemies of his race, fortified his country with strongholds, embellished it with temples, and with the superstructure of her fame laid the foundations of his own."[1] "Of the 84 fortresses for the defence of Mewar, 32 were erected by Kumbhá. He fortified the passes between the Western frontier of Mewar and Ábu and erected the fort of Vasanti. He founded Vasantapur[2] (v. 8) and built seven lakes near it in the vicinity of Anhalkund of Vashishta[2] in Sirohi (near Ábu). He built the fort of Machan to defend the Sherá Nullá and Devagarh against

[1] Annals and Antiquities of Rajasthan, Vol. I, p. 290.

[2] Chitorgarh *Kirtisthamba* Inscription.

the Mers of Aravalli. He built the fort of Kolana, near Amba Bhawani, and the fort of Vairat near Badnor, and rebuilt the fort of Áhore (in Mewar), which had been first built by his ancestor Karan Singh, and named it Kalash Meru. He built various other forts to overawe the Bhumiá Bhils of Jora and Panora, and defined the boundaries of Mewar and Marwar."[1]

## FORTS.

He constructed in 1452 A.D. (S. 1509, Magh Sudi 15th) a citadel on a peak of Mount Ábu, since well known as Achalagarh[2] within the fortress of the ancient Paramār kings of this country, where he often resided.

"The traveller would find the ruined towers of Achalgarh buried in the dense masses of cloud that surround him. The first pol (gate) of this ancient fortress is the Hanuman Pol, which is composed of two noble towers built with huge blocks of granite, black with the rude blasts of some 1,000

[1] Tod's Rajasthan, Vol. I, p. 290.

[2] Eklinga Mahatmya, Sl. 64 and the Chitorgarh Inscription, Plate XXI, Cunningham's A.S.R., Vol. XXIII.

winters. The towers had been connected at the top by a guard room, and the gate served as the entrance to the lower fort, whose dilapidated walls are discernable up the irregular ascent. Another portal called the Champa Pol, from a noble Champa tree close to it, which formerly denominated the "Gate of Wisdom," conducts to the inner fortress. The first object that strikes the view on passing the latter gate is the Jain temple to Paraswanath, erected at the sole expense of a banker of Māndoo. Its columns are of the same character as those of the ancient shrine of Ajmer.

"The upper fortress is attributed to Kumbha. But he probably only repaired this, the Donjon of Achalgarh, which, with the interior works, is of the most remote antiquity. There are the ruins of a granary, the *Bhandar* of Koombha Rana, coated within with a very strong cement. Close on the left is the palace of Oka Rani, his queen, so designated from being of Oka Mandal, near the Land's End of the Hindus. A small lake in the keep is called Sawan Bhadoon, and well merits the name of the two chief months of the monsoon, for in the middle of June it is yet full of water. On the most elevated knoll to the east are the remains of an alarm tower which still bears Kumbha's name. From this point the eye, occasionally piercing the swift scudding clouds, has glimpses of the ruined altars and palaces of the brave race who on the spot whence I surveyed them, had fought and bled in their defence."[1]

An equestrian statue of Rana Kumbhá with those of two other Maharanas and a bigger one of the Purohit or the family priest of Kumbha in a humble straw shed on the descent from Achalgarh to Dilwara still receive divine honours.

At Abu, Kumbha built the temple of Kumbhaswámi (which still stands) and a large tank named Ramakund in front of it.[2] He excavated four other tanks there.[2] He remitted the pilgrim tax levied at Abu.[2]

The highest monument of Kumbha's military and constructive genius, however, is

[1] Tod's Travels in Western Rajputana.

[2] Kumbha's Chitorgarh *Kirtistambha* Inscription (V. 12 and 13).

the wonderful fortress of Kumbhalgarh, or Kumbhalmer, second to none in strategical importance or historical renown. It was to this impregnable fortress that the Maharanas of Mewar always turned their eyes, when Udaipur became unsafe and Chitor untenable. It is to Kumbhalmer that every Maharana from Udai Singh to Ráj Singh sent the royal household when the entire might of the Mughal Empire was directed to the destruction of their country. It was the ambition of Akbar the Great to take it, when his hosts, led by the greatest of his generals, the renowed Raja Mán of Ámber and supported by the armies of the Rathors of Marwar, the Chohans of Sirohi, the Kuchhwahas of Amber (Jaipur) and other Rajput Chiefs, surrounded the country of the immortal Pratap.

The cunning of Akbar succeeded in raising against this devoted land all its Rajput neighbours, and the fortress fell. It was, however, recovered, and the successors of Akbar—Jahangir with all his vain glory, and Aurangzeb with all his craft and

Fortress of Kumbhalgarh

cunning,—failed to make any impression on this historic fortress. When Prince Khurrum, ennobled with the title of Shah Jahan (king of the world), with all the resources that the empire could command, supported by the Emperor Jahangir at the base of operations (Ajmer), overran the country of Pratap's noble son, Amra; or when that destroyer of the Moghul Empire, the great Aurangzeb, collecting the Imperial armies from all parts of the Empire, vainly launched his legions against the chivalrous Rana Raj Singh in an attempt to deprive this sacred soil of its ancient independence; this stronghold, the ever memorable Kumbhalgarh, provided shelter to those who were dear to the noble defenders of their fatherland. This fortress, which has played a part in history, seldom rivalled and never surpassed, was the bulwark of Mewar throughout the Mughal rule in India.

Kumbhalgarh and the *Kirtistambha* at Chitor are the two pillars on which the fame of Kumbha as a great commander and a great sovereign rests. Kumbhalgarh, situated in 25° 9′ N. and 73° 35′ E, about 60 miles north of Udaipur, stands on a high peak of the most westerly range of the Aravalli hills, on the site of an ancient stronghold, which, according to tradition, was built by the famous Jain King Samprati, who flourished in the second century of the Christian era. Kumbhá began the construction in S. 1500 (1443 A.D.) and it was completed in the dark half of *Chaitra* S. 1515[1] (A.D. 1458). The palace built by Kumbhá and rebuilt by the present Maharana stands 3,568 feet above sea level, and commands an extensive and fine view of the wild and rugged scenery of the Aravallis[2] and the sandy plains of Marwar. Below this peak on every side and enclosed within a high battlemented wall several feet thick, the uneven ground is studded with numerous old temples and reservoirs, barracks for the garrison, grain stores and other domed buildings. In the central open space of the fort, on a conical hillock, stands the inner

[1] Chitorgarh Inscription. Cunningham's Archæol: S. Reports, Vol. XXIII, plate 21.

[2] The names of the several neighbouring hills are given in the Chitorgarh Inscription as Nila, Shweta, Hemkut, Himvat, Nishad, Gandhamadan.

Katargarh and the *Vedi*

fort of Katárgarh. It is crowned with a palace called the *Jháli-ká-Máliá* or palace of the Jháli queen.

There are seven gates leading up to the fort. The principal (exterior) one, called the Hanumán Pol, from the image of the God which, with the gates, was brought by Kumbhá from Nagor and set up there, faces the south at the head of a road which winds gradually up through the gorge from the town of Kailwara at its base—a place of great historical interest. Between Kailwara and the Hanumán Pol there are two gates, the first being Áret Pol, or barrier thrown across the first narrow ascent about a mile from Kailwara. The second is called the Hulla Pol; the third is the Hanumán Pol, between which and the summit there are four more gates, *viz.*, the Gate of Victory, the Sanguinary Gate, the Gate of Ráma and the Chaugán Pol. Colonel James Tod says: "It would be vain to attempt describing the intricacies of approach to this far-famed abode, whose exterior is delineated by the pencil. A massive wall, with numerous towers and pierced battlements, having a strong resemblance to the Etruscan, encloses a space of some miles extent below, while the pinnacle or *Sikra* rises like the Crown of the Hindu Cybele, tier above tier of battlements, to the summit,[1] which is crowned with the *Badal Mahal* or 'Cloud Palace' of the Rana. Thence the eye ranges over the sandy deserts and the chaotic mass of mountains which are on all sides, covered with the cactus, which luxuriates amidst the rocks of the Aravalli."

Just inside the Hanumán Pol on the ridge below the palace is situated the Vedi, or the place where the *Yajna*, in consecration of the work, was performed by Kumbhá when the fort was completed. It is a beautiful three-storied building of great architectural merit; each tier is decorated with numerous massive low columns, resting on a sculptured panelled parapet and sustaining the roof of each storey, which being very low, admits but a broken light to break the pervading gloom.

[1] Tod's Annals and Antiquities of Rajasthan (original edition), Vol. I., page 670.

Fortress of Chitor and the Tower of Victory.

A memorable structure built by Rana Kumbhá in A.D. 1458 in the gorge below the fort on the brow of the mountain overlooking the pass, is the Mámádeva Temple. The court of the temple is formed by a strong wall enclosing a large area. The interior of this wall was covered with immense slabs of black marble, on which was inscribed the history of Mewar from the time of Guhil, the founder of the royal family, to Rana Kumbha.[1] Near this temple he built a large *Kunda* (reservoir of water), at the edge of which Kumbha was saying his prayers when he was treacherously stabbed by his son, Udá, the *Hatiáro* (parricide). Kumbhá built the Khumbhaswami Temple in the fort and constructed a lake by it.

## TOWER OF VICTORY.

Kumbha's *Jaya Stambha* (Tower of Victory), also called the *Kirtistambha* (Tower of Fame) in Chitorgarh is another monument of his genius and an ornament to that far-famed fortress. It was erected in A.D.

[1] Three of these slabs have since been removed to the Victoria Hall, Udaipur.

1448 to commemorate his victory over Sultan Mahmud Khilji of Malwa. And before it was completed in 1458 A.D.[1] Kumbha had triumphed over the combined armies of the kings of Gujrat and Malwa. Describing it, Mr. Fergusson says: "A pillar of victory like that of Trajan at Rome, but in infinitely better taste as an architectural object than the Roman example."[2]

Colonel James Tod[3] thus describes it: "The only thing in India to compare with this is the Kootab Minar at Delhi, but though much higher, it is of a very inferior character. This column is one hundred and twenty feet in height; the breadth of each face at the base is thirty-five feet, and at the summit, immediately under the cupola, seventeen feet and a half. It stands on an ample terrace, forty-two feet square. It has nine distinct storeys, with openings at every face of each storey, and all these doors have colonnaded porticos." A

[1] The Chitorgarh Inscription (A. S. R., Vol. XXIII., plate 21) gives the date as Thursday, the Sudh 10th of Magh, Pushiya Nakhshtra, S. 1505.

[2] History of Indian and Eastern Architecture, page 253.

[3] Annals and Antiquities of Rajasthan, Vol. II., page 761.

stair in the centre communicates with each and leads to the two upper storeys, which are open and more ornamental than those below. The whole of the lower is covered with architectural ornaments and sculptures to such an extent as to leave no plain parts, while at the same time this mass of decoration is kept so subdued that it in no way interferes either with the outline or the general effect of the pillar. "It is built chiefly of compact limestone and the quartz rock on which it stands, which takes the highest polish: indeed there are portions possessing the hardness, and exhibiting the fracture, of Jasper. It is one mass of sculpture; of which a better idea cannot be conveyed than in the remark of those who dwell about it, that it contains every object known to their mythology. The ninth *khand* or 'storey' which, as I have stated, is seventeen feet and a half square, has numerous columns supporting a vault, in which is sculptured Kanaya in the *Rasmandala* (celestial sphere), surrounded by the *gopis*, or muses, each holding a musical instrument, and in a dancing attitude. Beneath this is a richly-carved scroll fringed with the *sarus*, the *phenicopteros* of ornithology. Around this chamber had been arranged, on black marble[1] tablets, the whole genealogy of the Ranas of Chitor; but the Goths have broken or defaced all save one slab." "Who could look," asks Col. Tod, "on this lovely, this majestic column, which tells in language more easy of interpretation than the tablets within, of

'.........deeds which should not pass away,
And names which must not wither,'

and withold a sigh for its departed glories?"

Colonel Tod further says: "The view from this elevated spot was superb, extend-

[1] A copy of this and the Kumbhalgarh Inscription of Rana Kumbha was taken by a pandit on *Phagun Vadi* 7th, S. 1735 (A.D. 1679), when five tablets of this, and one of the Kumbhalgarh Inscriptions were in existence. Unfortunately only two tablets of this former Inscription are now to be found, but two more tablets and a fragment of the third of the Kumbhalgarh Inscription have been recovered. The Kumbhalgarh Inscription originally consisted of five tablets and the Chitorgarh of seven or more. The Chitorgarh Inscription states that it was completed on Monday the Margshir Vadi 5th, S. 1517 and Saka year 1382 (A.D. 1460). The author of the Inscription was a Brahman named Atri, who was well versed in Logic, Vedanta, Veda, Mimansa and Sahitya. He was the son of Keshava, called Jhoting, and grandson of Narahari and great grandson of Somanath of the Bhragu family.

ing far into the plains of Malwa. The lightning struck and injured the dome[1] some years ago, but generally there is no semblance of decay, though some shoots of *peepul* have rooted themselves where the bolt of Indra fell. It is said to have cost ninety lakhs of rupees, or near a million sterling, and this is only one of the many magnificent works of Rana Kumbha within Chitor, the temples to Krishna, the lake called Cooram Sagar, the temple[2] and fountain to Kookereoo (Kukreshwar), Mahadeva having been erected by him."

Kumbha strengthened the defences of Chitor[3] and built seven of its gates—the Rámpol, after Ráma the great hero of the solar dynasty; the Hanumánpol, called after the temple of this god; the Bhairavapol,

[1] The old injured dome was removed and the present bulbous dome constructed by Maharana Swarup Singh after A.D. 1839.

[2] This temple was originally built by Raja Kukreshwar, who excavated the fountain in A.D. 755 (Magh Sud 5th S. 811 (Thursday).—Archæological Survey Report, Vol. XXIII, p. 113.

[3] The Chitorgarh *Kirtistambha* Inscription, verse 42. Verse 183 says that in *Kartik* S. 1507 (A.D. 1450) Kumbha built a new bastion with battlements.

since called after Bhairavadás Solankhi, who fought bravely and was killed at that spot in the battle against Bahadur Shah of Gujrat in A.D. 1534-35; and Lakshmipol, Chamundápol, Tárápol and Rájpol.[1] Kumbha built at Chitor the magnificent temple of Kumbhaswami, "which was like the crown of the world."[2] This temple stands to the south of the *Badá Mahal* and is mentioned as the temple of Govind Shyam by Abul Fazal in his Akbarnama. It was built[3] by Kumbha in S. 1505 (A.D. 1448). By its side Maharana Kumbha built the temple of Ádi Varaha, which is now wrongly called *Miranbái's* temple. He also built a Ráma Kund[4] at Chitor. Midway between the *Nava Lakhá Bhandar* and the *Nava Kothá*, built by the imposter Banbir in A.D. 1537, and near the Tower of Victory stands the "graceful

[1] The last four pols are now known as Lakshmanapol, Jorlápol, Ganeshapol and Padalpol.

[2] Commentary on *Gita Govind*, Shloka 63.

[3] According to Tod, this temple was constructed from wrecks of more ancient shrines brought from the ruins of a city of remote antiquity called *Nagari*, six miles north of Chitor.

[4] The well-known lake *Rama Kund* at Jāwar (Mewar) was built in 1497 A.D. by Kumbha's daughter, Ramābāi, who had been married to Raja Mandalik of Girnar.

Temple of Ranpur.

and richly-carved"[1] building called the *Singar Chauri* or *Vedi*, built by Bhandari Bela, son of Sáh Kolá, Treasurer to Maharana Kumbha in S. 1505 (A.D. 1448-49).

Rana Kumbha built the present road[2] up the hill by which carriages can go up to the fort. Before his time there was only a foot-path.

## TEMPLES.

Though the temple of Kumbha Shyam at Chitorgarh is a noteworthy one, yet of all the temples erected or resuscitated in his time, the temple of Ranpur is the most important. It was erected in the Sadri Pass leading from the western descent of the highlands of Mewar, and is dedicated to Rishabnath or Rishabdeva, the first of the Jaina *Tirthankaras*. It is situated in a spot evidently selected for its natural beauties. Its foundations were laid in A.D. 1438 by the Rana's favourite architect, Dharnak.[3] It consists of three stories and is supported

[1] Archæol. S. Reports, Vol. XXIII, p. 118.
[2] The Chitorgarh *Kirtistambha* Inscription.
[3] Archæological Survey of India: Annual Report for 1907-8, p. 217.

by numerous columns of granite upwards of forty feet in height. The interior is inlaid with mosaics of cornelian and agate. "It is one of the largest edifices existing, and cost upwards of a million sterling, towards which Kumbha contributed eighty thousand pounds."[1]

Mr. Fergusson says that Maharana Kumbha, "during his long and prosperous reign filled his country with beautiful buildings, both civil and ecclesiastical. Amongst others he built this temple of Sadri, situated in a lonely and deserted glen, running into the western slope of the Aravalli, below his favourite fort of Kumbhalgarh. Notwithstanding long neglect, it is still nearly perfect, and is the most complicated and extensive Jaina temple I have myself ever had an opportunity of inspecting."

"From the plan (woodcut No. 133) it would be perceived that it is nearly a square, 200 ft. by 225 ft., exclusive of the projections on each face. In the centre stands the great shrine, not, however, occupied, as usual, by one cell, but by four; or rather four great niches, in each of which

[1] Tod's Rajasthan, Vol. I, p. 289.

is placed a statue of Adinatha, or Rishabdeva, the first and greatest of the Jaina saints. Above this are four other niches, similarly occupied, opening on the terraced roofs of the building. Near the four angles of the court are four smaller shrines, and around them, or on each side of them, are 20 domes supported by about 420 columns; 4 of these domes—the central ones of each group—are 3 storeys in height, and tower over the others; and one—that facing the principal entrance—is supported by the very unusual number of 16 columns, and is 36 ft. in diameter, the others being only 24 ft. Light is admitted to the building by four uncovered courts, and the whole is surrounded by a range of cells, many of them now unoccupied, each of which has a pyramidal roof of its own. The internal effect of this forest of columns may be gathered from the view (woodcut 143) taken across one of its courts; but it is impossible that any view can reproduce the endless variety of perspective and the play of light and shade which results from the disposition of the pillars and of the domes, and from the mode in which the light is introduced. A wonderful effect also results from the number of cells, most of them containing images of *Tirthankars*, which everywhere meet the view. Besides the twelve in the central Sikhars, there are eighty-six cells of very varied form and size surrounding the interior, and all their façades more or less adorned with sculpture............ Indeed, I know of no other building in India of the same class that leaves so pleasing an impression or affords so many hints for the graceful arrangement of columns in an interior.

"Besides its merits of design, its dimensions are by no means to be despised; it covers altogether about 48,000 square ft., or nearly as much as one of our ordinary Mediæval Cathedrals; and, taking the basement into account, is nearly of equal bulk; while in amount of labour and of sculptural decorations it far surpasses any."[1]

Maharana Kumbhá renovated the famous temple of Eklingaji in Mewar and constructed

[1] History of Indian and Eastern Architecture, pp. 241-244.

the magnificent *Kumbha Mandapa* in front of the *sanctum sanctorum.* He built the surrounding wall and presented the temple with its gold flagstaff and *kalas.*

He bestowed on the temple four villages, named Nagda, Kathdawan, Amalkhera and Bhiman (Bhuvana).

Eklingji is the Cathedral town of Mewar, and the Rana, like the ancient Buddhist king of Gāndhāra, is the Defender of the Faith and the Head of the Church. It is situated in a defile about 14 miles north of Udaipur. The road, which has recently been improved, passes over undulating hills, particularly along a valley and over a gorge about two-thirds of the way, beyond which it is more level and surrounded by a number of small lakes which beautify the country. The temple is dedicated to Mahádeva or Ishvara. A four-faced image was placed in the temple in Sambat 1545 (A.D. 1488). Nandi (bull), the steed of god, is here represented by a life-size brazen statue.

Early in the 8th century the sage

Hárita conferred on Bappá Ráwal the title of Regent of Eklingji, and to this day the Maharanas of Mewar, as Diwáns or Regents of Siva, supersede the high priest in his duties and themselves perform the ceremonies when they visit the temple.

Early in the fifteenth century Maharana Mokal rebuilt the edifice which the Muhammadans had destroyed. The temple is of unusual design, having a double-storied porch and a double-storied sanctuary, the former covered by a flat pyramidal roof composed of many hundred circular knobs, the latter roofed by a lofty tower of more than ordinary elaboration.

The town of Eklingji is separated from Nagda by a lake, which is one of the many artificial waters that beautify the Udaipur valley, and its *bund* or dam was built by Bhogaditya five generations before Bappa, and has since been frequently repaired. It is shut in by wooded hills and on its western margin are two interesting temples, both ranking high as specimens of ancient Hindu architecture.

# CHAPTER X.

## Kumbha as a Scholar.

Great as Kumbhá was as a sovereign and a commander, he was equally great as a scholar and a poet. The Kumbhalgarh Inscription says that it was as easy for him to write poetry as it was to go to battle. It is marvellous how, while constantly engaged in warfare, defending his empire against his foes, conquering new territories and adding them to Mewar, building forts, strengthening the defences of the country, embellishing it with works of art, continually moving from one part of the country to another, the Maharana could find opportunities to develop his literary abilities and time to write poetry, compose dramas, annotate old poems and write treatises on the Science of Music.

He was an accomplished musician and possessed a knowledge of the science, unequalled in his time. He was regarded as the highest authority on music; and because of this, the title of *Abhinava Bharatácharya* (new Bharatácharya), as distinguished from the old Bharatácharya, the authority on *Nátya Shastra* in ancient India, was conferred on him.

His works on music, *Sangitarája*,[1] *Sangita Mimánsá*[1] and *Rasika Priyá* (commentary on the celebrated lyric *Gita Govinda*)[2] and his commentary on *Sangita Ratnakar* are evidence of his mastery of the science.

Other works known to have been written by him are four dramas and a commentary on *Chandi Shataka*.[2] The important contemporary work, *Eklinga Mahátmya*, shows that Rana Kumbhá knew the Vedas[3] and was well versed in the *Smrities* (law).

[1] Chitorgarh Inscription. See also Catalogue of Mss. existing in the Central Provinces by F. Keilhorn, Nagpur, 1874 A.D.

[2] Chitorgarh *Kirthistambha* Inscription.

[3] The Chitorgarh Inscription says that in his four dramas he made use of Karnátaki, Medapáti and Mahárásbtri languages, and adds that in *Nátaka (play par excellence) Prakarana* (play that takes a less elevated range than *Nataka*) *Vithi* (one act play performed by one or two actors) *Natiká* (a play in 4 acts), *Bhán* (monologue in one act), *Prahasana* (farcical or comical satire in one act), *Rupaka* (drama generally) he was a new Bharata.

*Mimánsá* (philosophy), *Natya Shastra* (dramatic writings.) *Rajaniti* (polity), *Ganita* (mathematics); *Vyakarana* (grammar), *Upnishads* and *Tarka* (logic.) He knew the Karnátaki, the Maharáshtri and other languages. The commentary on Gita Govinda, named *Rasika Priyá* and the last part of *Eklinga Mahátmya*, which was written by Kumbhá himself, show that he was a great Sanskrit scholar, and that he wrote good poetry with as much ease as prose. The former work contains quotations from numerous Sanskrit works and shows that Kumbhá was a man of extensive reading. The last part of *Eklinga Mahátmya* is a lyric, and its poetry is sweet and musical, and full of grace and beauty. The *Eklinga Mahátmya* (sloka 74) mentions four dramas[1] written by him. This would show that he was a scholar of *Prákrita*, like the famous Chohan Emperor Visaladeva; but, as none of his plays has so far been discovered, it is neither possible to speak of his proficiency in the *Prákrita* nor to assign him a place due to him amongst the dramatists of India.

[1] Chitorgarh *Kirtistambha* Inscription.

Himself a great scholar, Rana Kumbha always valued men of learning, and showed them respect and appreciation. He took great interest in architecture, as is clear from the magnificent buildings and works of art constructed during his time in Mewar—at Chitor, Ábu, Kumbhalgarh, Ránpur and other places. A number of books on this noble art were written under his auspices, some of which have come to light. The following eight books on architecture and sculpture were written by Rana Kumbha's architect Mandan (see Abfrecht's Catalogue Catalogorum, part I., pp. 730-I.)

(१) देवतामूर्त्तिप्रकरण। (५) वास्तुमंडन।
(२) प्रासादमंडन। (६) वास्तुशास्त्र।
(३) राजवल्लभ। (७) वास्तुसार।
(४) रूपमंडन। (८) रूपावतार।

Three other works, उद्धारधोरणी, कलानिधि, द्वारदीपिका, by Mandan's son, Govind, and वास्तुमंजरी, by Mandan's brother, Náthá, are in existence at Udaipur and were seen with Champálal, a descendant of Mandan, by Prof. S. R. Bhandarkar, as mentioned by him in his "Report of a second tour in search of Sanskrit manuscripts in Rajputana and Central India in 1904-6 A.D."

Rana Kumbhá had a work on the subject of *Kirtistambha* (Tower of Fame), written by one of his architects, and had it engraved on stone tablets. A part of the first tablet, found at Chitor and since deposited in the Udaipur Museum, says that the work was written under the orders of Maharana Kumbhá.

---